Case Studies for the General Public in Hypnosis and Medical Hypnoanalysis

Case Studies for the General Public in Hypnosis and Medical Hypnoanalysis

Jules Leeb

Rev. date: 10/17/2016

To order additional copies of this book, contact:
Xlibris
1-800-455-039
www.Xlibris.com.au
Orders@Xlibris.com.au
751492

Table of Contents

Dedication

This book is dedicated to the thousands of women, men, boys and girls who entrusted me with their 'emotional well-being'.

I also dedicate this book to my wonderful wife, Marion, who has been my best friend for over 60 years.

Foreword

I have known Dr Jules Leeb for so many years – since my medical student days – being guided and enlightened by him when he was an obstetrics/gynaecology resident. There followed a decades-long friendship and professional relationship which included him introducing me to Clinical Hypnosis and specifically Medical Hypnoanalysis (MHA).

My first reaction to his suggestion that I explore the subject was one of disbelief – I was fixed in the 2+2=4 thinking of genetics and biochemistry. What convinced me was a shared patient who required surgery, a patient truly phobic about surgical procedures, whom I had promised to be present for her operation since she'd had otherwise have refused the anaesthetic let alone surgery. Outside the operating theatre I found her with eyes closed and utterly at peace. About to announce my presence to her Jules gently said 'leave her be, she's in trance'. I checked her notes thinking they'd overdosed her with morphine for with previous surgery she'd be climbing the walls in a frantic effort to escape by now. Her charts showed no sedation at all. I was hooked.

That began an amazing journey for me and my patients to the extent I withdrew from family practice and instead have been using this wonderful modality of MHA for more than 25 years without regret but with huge fulfilment. From anxiety to depression, from migraine and asthma to the autoimmune disorders such as lupus … from dark confusion we moved forward to clarity in Light … to healing.

Jules was for many years a valued teacher of Clinical Hypnosis for our South African Society of Clinical Hypnosis, a Division of the Psychological Society of South Africa.

Dr Leeb presents his cases in his usual candid yet heartfelt manner. He demonstrates that we all have power, we have control of our destiny, we can choose how to think, how to feel and how to behave. All we need is guidance.

Read … believe and be in awe.

Dr Trevor Modlin

Johannesburg, South Africa

Introduction

This book describes patients treated by Hypnosis during the past 36 years. This is not a medical text book. It is being written so that lay people will have a better understanding of hypnosis and particularly of "Medical Hypnoanalysis".

I will discuss hypnosis in such a way that readers will have a better understanding of what hypnosis is.

Hypnosis is not sleep. It is not losing control. Nor is it having your mind taken over. You will never say or do anything you don't want to do.

My favourite definition of hypnosis is, that it is **"A state of profound relaxation in which the body sleeps and the mind is wide-awake"**.

The mind is more **awake** than usual. The senses are heightened. One can hear better, see better, smell better and taste better than usual.

I'm often asked by colleagues if I would be prepared to hypnotise someone who has been to numerous hypnotherapists, but has failed to be hypnotised.

When the patient arrives, and we start talking, the first question I ask is, "Did the therapist explain hypnosis to you?"

Usually, the answer is, "No".

If hypnosis is not explained, the majority of patients would say something like "thanks for trying Doc, but nothing happened. I was wide-awake and heard everything".

The process would **not** have met his or her expectations.

Most expect to be *"asleep"*, and to have no memory of what happened. Nothing can be further from the truth.

Unless informed of what to expect, very few would believe that they had been hypnotised.

No one knows exactly where the mind is, but it is generally accepted that it is in the brain. Similarly, it is not known exactly where the conscious and unconscious minds are, but we accept and visualise them as separate and in constant communication with each other. The conscious mind is awareness.

When one studies the knowledge is stored very much like on a computer hard drive, and is available when required.

Only 20% of what is stored in the unconscious mind passes through the conscious mind. The rest of the information goes directly through into the unconscious mind without conscious awareness.

We have learned from experience that in hypnosis we are able to communicate with the unconscious mind.

In hypnosis the mind behaves like a computer waiting to be programmed. The left brain, which is the logical brain in right-handed people, is in 'neutral' and able to accept suggestions. The right brain is the creative brain.

Under normal circumstances if I press 6+6 on my computer keyboard the answer will be 12. If I were able to program, I could program my computer that the answer would be 45. In the same way, when logical thought is suspended, as it is in hypnosis, the suggestions work the same way. When a suggestion is accepted, it is accepted as if it was your idea and not mine. You will never accept suggestions that are in conflict with your morality code.

I assure you that no well-trained therapist would give you suggestions that could embarrass or compromise you.

There are no dangers in hypnosis. You do need to trust the person you working with. The same dangers exist as would exist in any doctor–patient relationship.

You will never say or do anything that you do not want to do, but you may remember things you cannot otherwise remember. Those of us who practice Medical Hypnoanalysis believe that experiences throughout life are stored in the unconscious mind, and become available in hypnosis.

After explaining hypnosis, I ask if he or she believes that they will be cured by my giving them direct suggestions. Most would say no, and they would be correct.

The conscious mind is a very clever mind. It knows what it wants but it does not know how to do it. In addition, it can only do one thing at a time.

The unconscious mind, however, can do hundreds of things at the same time.

If you wish to bend a finger, or to smile, the unconscious mind produces a number of chemicals which cause joints to bend and the muscles to contract.

When you go to bed at night you don't have to think, "I hope my heart beats", because your unconscious mind does this automatically. It is the same when you sit in a bright light and your pupils constrict. When the light is dim, your pupils open.

Your unconscious mind is concerned with your **survival**, and it will do anything for you to survive. It believes that you need your symptoms, and that if you did not have them, something worse may happen.

Our job, yours and mine, is to find out what it is protecting you from.

This is done by a process called "Medical Hypnoanalysis".

It is called **Medical** Hypnoanalysis because it follows the medical model of taking a history, and making a likely diagnosis from the history. Further tests are done to either, exclude or include, other possible diagnoses. Finally, a diagnosis is made.

The "emotional abscess" is identified, drained and removed. The patient is rehabilitated much the same as the case of a surgical abscess would be treated.

The foundation of Medical Hypnoanalysis is the "Triple Allergenic Theory".

The triple allergenic theory states that one does not have a severe allergic response to the first exposure to an antigen. The first exposure creates antibodies. The second exposure increases antibodies and results in mild symptoms. The third and subsequent exposures may result in severe reactions.

An antigen is any substance that causes the immune system to produce antibodies against it. The immune system does not recognise the substance and is trying to fight it off.

In Medical Hypnoanalysis the antigen is the unconscious perception of an emotion.

Fear, Anxiety, Guilt, Anger and other emotions are the antigens that create emotional antibodies.

Let me explain this in a simple way. The body protects itself against foreign matter. But not all foreign matter is harmful to all people.

Usually, penicillin does no harm to the machinery of the body.

Even if there is a genetic predilection to be allergic to penicillin, the first time it is injected the amount is too small to cause much damage and the body manages to get rid of it with a bit of a struggle.

The body makes a careful note of the event, and creates a few 'bullets' to keep just in case the 'pest' shows up again. Penicillin, in this scenario would be the 'Antigen'. The 'Bullets' would be the 'Antibodies'.

If penicillin, is injected again sometime later, even years later, the 'bullets' get rid of it again. But this second episode added to the first one causes *some damage. The* body now prepares something more powerful, *like a Bomb.* [more antibodies].

"The body/immune system, says something like, "if that bugger shows up again, I will blast him to kingdom come".

With the next injection of penicillin that bomb that had been so carefully prepared and stored carefully away, sometimes for many years, is brought out and it works. The penicillin is instantly destroyed but the collateral damage is enormous – it is called an "Allergic response".

Since it takes *three episodes* for the whole thing to play out, it is called the 'Triple Allergic Response'

Medical Hypnoanalysis seems to work in a similar way.

Hence, "the Triple Allergenic Response theory".

The above scenario explains "antigen" and "antibodies".

When someone presents with a problem, it is considered as if it were a *weed* in a garden.

A weed has a seed, a root and many branches.

Because the triple allergenic response is regarded as the cause of all problems, it is important that there is a full understanding of it.

The following should serve as an excellent example to provide complete clarification.

A patient is asked to imagine that I've taken a strawberry from the refrigerator, and given him/her one.

After eating it, he or she, may develop a severe anaphylactic reaction. After resuscitation, I would enquire as to why I was not informed about the allergy to strawberries.

Usually the response is, "I have never had a strawberry before".

Based on the "Triple allergenic response theory" it is not possible to have such a response, unless one had previously been exposed to strawberries. In this scenario the strawberry is the antigen.

This event, where a severe reaction occurs for the first time is called a "*Symptom Intensifying Event*".

The antibodies would have increased to a level where severe symptoms or anaphylaxis may occur.

In the Medical Hypnoanalysis model the antibodies would be '*psychological antibodies*'.

From this time onwards every time the patient is exposed to a strawberry, the symptoms will recur and become gradually worse. After a while, even touching a strawberry may result in the same response.

Even later, seeing a photograph of a strawberry may have the same effect.

When enquiring from their parents as to when they had their first strawberry, the parent would usually say something like, "when you were five years old we were visiting on a farm and the lady gave you a strawberry. You developed a rash on your thumb". This could not be the first exposure, because there was a rash on the thumb. Some antibodies must have already been present.

This event is called a *"Symptom Producing Event"*.

On subsequent enquiry from the parent, the patient may be told that they had never had a strawberry before.

That would probably be correct.

The father may have bought his wife a strawberry ice cream just before she went into labour, and when the patient suckled on her breast, he or she would have been exposed to strawberry, and would begin to produce antibodies.

This is called *"The Initial Sensitising Event"*.

It is never consciously remembered. It is in the unconscious mind and is the *"seed"* of the problem. If not found and neutralised, the symptom cannot be relieved.

There are a number of essential 'Tools' in Medical Hypnoanalysis.

The first is the *"Word Association Exercise"*. *(The special investigations)*.

The second tool is *"Regression"*. (Exploration).

Regression, going back in time, is the essence of the therapy. It is believed by those who practice medical hypnoanalysis, that memories are stored at a subconscious level and become available in hypnosis.

During the word association exercise, the unconscious mind is asked to respond to words and phrases. The responses guide the therapist in the search for the initial sensitising event, symptom producing event and symptom intensifying events.

The analogy of the "Tuning Forks"

If there are a number of tuning forks set to vibrate at a particular frequency, and one is 'pinged' the others would also vibrate. It is called spatial reverberation in physics.

In Medical Hypnoanalysis, the emotion of an experience, like the tuning forks, vibrates back to the initial emotion.

Medical hypnoanalysis is not as much concerned with the events in a patient's life, as it is concerned with the *emotion* that the event created.

"When X came to see me he had been suffering from severe depression and guilt.

He started feeling guilty after he had divorced his wife.

The guilt became progressively worse and eventually he became severely depressed.

No one was able to cure him.

No one could understand why he was still feeling so guilty.

He and his ex-wife were good friends.

They were both remarried, and they often went out as a foursome!

He had consulted many therapists and psychiatrists, but no one could help him.

It did not make sense that he should still feel so guilty.

After taking his complete history, hypnosis was induced and the "Word Association Exercise" was completed.

Regressions followed.

The first memory was a feeling of guilty for not being able to help a friend who committed suicide. He was 19 years old.

This guilt had nothing to do with leaving his wife, but the emotion, 'guilt', was the same.

Next he regressed to the age of 12. He had stolen a fountain pen from a news agency. He felt guilty.

When he was four he felt guilty for having kicked his pet dog.

Finally, he regressed to being born by Caesarean section, and said, "I have killed my mother".

The subconscious perception of the newborn baby was that his mother was dead The caesarean section was done under general anaesthetic.

According to the *analogy of the tuning forks*, when he left his wife, the guilt "vibrated" back to the original guilt (his birth) and he developed symptoms.

This was the initial sensitising event.

The Symptom producing event was at the age of 4.

The symptom intensifying events were at 12 and 19. The last straw was when he left his wife.

The cure was to convince the unconscious mind to accept the fact that his mother had not died, and that his perception was incorrect.

When this was accepted, he was cured.

In hypnosis, the word "sleep" is often used.

Similarly, the word "awake" is used.

However, the patient is never asleep and is more awake than usual.

We use the words "sleep" and "awake" because they are convenient words to use.

The importance of a detailed history.

When taking a history one attempts to write down the first three sentences verbatim.

This includes observation of non-verbal cues.

The first three sentences are regarded as important, because they often reveal the diagnosis, either partially or in full.

When the patient leaves home for therapy, the unconscious mind does not 'remain behind', and during the history the unconscious often leaks information by using certain words or by non-verbal communication.

When asked what the problem was, Joan said,

"Headaches. As long as I can remember. I have always had them since I was 12".

In this particular case the treatment was completed in two sessions.

'As long as I can remember' suggest the possibility of an event at about the age of three.

'Always' suggested something occurred before birth.

'Since I was 12' was the Symptom Intensifying Event, 'The last straw'.

The "Initial Sensitizing Event" was before birth.

Symptom Producing Event was about the age of 3.

Regression to those particular ages, reliving the experiences, and 'reframing the memories', resulted in removing them from the unconscious mind, and hence cure.

Reframing.

Reframing is a way of reviewing experiences. events, ideas, concepts and emotions, to find more positive alternatives.

Reframing is achieved in numerous ways.

Firstly, it may be done using 'cognitive restructuring' (logical explanation).

It may also be achieved by asking an older part of the personality to communicate with the younger part, thereby assisting in changing the subconscious perception. Asking the older part to give the younger part information that it did not have at that particular age, is very effective in reframing experiences.

<u>*Perception.*</u>

Perception is the way in which something is regarded, understood, or interpreted.

The unconscious cannot distinguish fact from fiction.

If the unconscious accepts an experience, suggestion or emotion, it is accepted as if it were indeed *the truth, even if it is not so.*

When the unconscious mind and the conscious mind are in conflict, the unconscious always wins.

The imagination is more powerful than the will.

We are 'prisoners' of our perceptions.

For example, if I open the front door to invite someone in, and he or she looks at me, and thinks, "He does not like me", that would be the perception. He or she will behave toward me as if I did not like them. Soon I would really not like them.

I will describe the other "tools" that are used as I discuss the cases.

Although I will concentrate on "Medical Hypnoanalysis", I will also describe patients treated by "Traditional Hypnotherapy" and "Ego State therapy".

Ego states manifest in a 'family of self' within a single individual.

You may have had the experience of looking at something in a shop window and thinking, "I would like to buy that". A part of you pops up and says "do not be silly, you cannot afford it". Another part may pop up and say "well, if you sell your car?". Eventually, the most reasonable part pops up and says, "forget about it. Let us go home".

Diagnosis.

Conscious diagnosis.

Unconscious diagnosis.

The *conscious diagnosis* is the one that the patient presents with — the symptom. Fear, Anxiety, Depression, Anger, Loss of self-esteem and Guilt are most frequent presenting problems.

The *unconscious diagnosis* refers to the cause of the problem at an emotional level.

The unconscious diagnoses in hypnoanalysis are the following: –

Jurisdictional Problem. (Guilt complex).

Identity problem – being the wrong person, unwanted, and perhaps the wrong sex.

Walking Zombie Syndrome – refers to when the unconscious mind has accepted the concept of death, either physical or emotional (walking zombie syndrome spiritual). The unconscious mind has accepted that death has occurred, may occur or is imminent.

Separation Anxiety Syndrome – being separated from a parent, a loved one, spirituality and lack of self-love.

Ponce De Leon Syndrome –refers to someone who for some reason, is stuck "in the Fountain of youth", and behaves and responds as if they were still young or, wanted to be young.

An example, could be a 45-year-old woman dressed like a 13-year-old, and behaving as if she were.

Prenatal experience. – refers to experiences and perceptions inside mother's womb

Birth experience – refers to the subjective experience of the baby during the birth process and, includes the "Birth Anoxia Syndrome" which refers to the experience of impending death during birth.

There is usually a *Dominant* syndrome, but there are often elements of some of the other syndromes present. This will become evident during the case discussions.

This book will be devoted to the discussion of clinical patients that have been treated by me over the years.

Attempted Suicide

Alice was referred by her psychiatrist. She had attempted suicide while in hospital. He found her lying in a pool of blood with both her wrists slashed. When I asked what the problem was she said, "I want to die". She said the problem started when her father died. He died suddenly when she was 10 years old. She was not allowed to attend his funeral. She had been the apple of his eye. She never had a chance to say goodbye. When he died, she died emotionally. She had been trying to kill herself ever since. She begged God to allow her to be with her father, but she was constantly disappointed. She was often hospitalised. Lately, her depression had become so bad that she was given electroconvulsive therapy on numerous occasions. There was very little benefit from the treatment. As a result of her emotional state her husband and children were having problems. Their sex life had always been perfect, but there had been no sexual contact for the past year.

She described her childhood as scary, because her father had always been ill. Her father died at the age of 41. She never had a good relationship with her mother because she was not in any way affectionate and there were constant 'mind games'. She wished her mother would have been softer, affectionate and more honest.

As a result of a dispute with her siblings about her mother's will, she has not spoken with her elder sister or her brother for a long-time. She has a good relationship with her second sister.

She had her first "nervous breakdown" when she was 17.

When she was three she was very ill, and her parents and the doctor thought that she may die.

She often felt as if she were about eight years old.

She was unhappy in primary school because the other children teased her by saying "you don't have a daddy". She was terribly unhappy in high school until she was transferred to a private school where she felt happy for the first time.

When asked what she thought people said about her behind her back that she did not like, she said, "they are frustrated with me".

If she could change anything about herself, it would be her death wish.

Hypnosis was easily induced.

The Word Association Exercise, was valuable in deciding where to look for the initial sensitising event.

Regressions.

Prenatal experience.

She felt as if she was full-term in her mother's womb and wanting to get out because it was not safe anymore. There was pressure on her chest and she complained of tightness and 'smoke'. There was no love or warmth and she felt as if she did not belong there. This was the initial sensitising event for the *'Spiritual walking zombie syndrome'*, the *'Ponce De Leon syndrome'* and the *'Jurisdictional problem'*.

The Prenatal experience was reframed using the 47-year-old ego state, and by giving her direct suggestions. A script, "Life the purpose is you" was worked through. She was tremendously relieved by the experience. It referred to her having the right to be here.

When she returned she was feeling somewhat better.

The next experience occurred just after birth. There was a feeling of hurt, anger and guilt. She felt guilty for being here because she was unwanted, and was the wrong sex. She felt that her mother was disappointed that she had another girl.

This was the initial sensitising event for the *'identity problem'*, and the symptom producing event for the *'Jurisdictional problem'*.

The next experience occurred at the age of four. She was in a freezing cold bath. She thought she would die. This was, however, an incorrect perception. The reason for the cold bath was because she had had a high fever. This experience was reframed and she accepted that there had been no harm intended.

When she was six years old she had a tonsillectomy and felt abandoned because her parents had left her in the hospital, and they were not allowed to visit her. However, when they brought her home and showered her with presents, she felt better. She was allowed to sleep in their bed. It was easy to reframe this experience.

In Medical Hypnoanalysis, it is not necessary to look at every experience in a person's life. One needs to find the *initial sensitising event*, the *symptom producing event*, and a few *symptom intensifying events*. When these have been worked through and reframed healing can begin.

This is why Medical hypnoanalysis is described as '*short-term and directed therapy*'.

The next relevant experience occurred at the age of 10. The death of her father.

A script wherein she was to imagine being with her father, and telling him how she missed him and loved him, was introduced. She was to listen to what he had to say to her. They spent some time together and soon it was time to say goodbye.

On her wedding day, her mother and brother expressed their dislike of the man she was marrying. This spoilt what should have been a wonderful day.

All these experiences were reframed.

Ideomotor exploration.

Ideomotor exploration is a way of communicating with the unconscious mind in hypnosis. The unconscious mind is asked to identify a finger in the dominant hand that would represent "*yes*", another to represent '*no*', another to represent "*I would like to talk with you*" and one to represent "*I do not want to tell you*". When the unconscious mind agrees to do something, or to go to a particular experience, or to respond in some other way, it is suggested that the 'yes finger' will lift. The other fingers respond accordingly.

Her problem was described as a '*weed* 'growing in the corner of the garden of her mind. The weed was draining all the goodness from the garden and as a result she could see how desolate the garden looked. The grass was brown, the flowers had lost their colour and the shrubs were all shrivelled up. She was told that this weed had been planted from a seed planted a long time ago. Sometime later, the root began to grow, and eventually large branches grew. The seed was the initial sensitising event, the root was a symptom producing event and the branches were all symptom intensifying events. These events had all been identified during the regressions. She was asked whether she was ready to remove the weed from her mind. It took some time to do, but eventually she pulled it out and was asked to destroy it by burning it. She can see how healthy the garden now was. She was told to sit in the garden for a while and to enjoy looking at it. There was a large hole where the weed was, and she planted a strong tree in its place.

Following the removal of the weed, she was given suggestions about returning to life and living again. She was pleased.

At the next session she informed me that she had been socialising; something she had not done for a long time, and that she was happy within herself. There was no suicidal ideation.

She was taught how to "*reject negative suggestions*" coming from her own thoughts and from the words of others.

At the following session, she brought with her a diary she had kept while she was in hospital. She wondered whether we should read it. I suggested it would be best to destroy it and never think of it again. She agreed, and it was destroyed in her presence.

A script in which she was to *"believe you are alive"* was done and was followed by suggestions to give her confidence.

The suggestion that her mind was now going to heal her automatically was implanted by reading a script, *'automatic healing'*.

To complete the removal of the Ponce DeLeon syndrome aspect of her problem, she was asked **to fantasise an ideal childhood** —a childhood she wished she had had. She was to indicate 'yes' when she was able to do so and was satisfied with the fantasised childhood.

When she did, via ideomotor signals the unconscious mind was asked whether it would be willing to store the fantasised childhood as a true memory. There was an agreement. She was then informed that 'now and in the future you will find yourself behaving, acting and reacting as if the fantasised memory was the actual memory of your childhood.

The process was completed in eight sessions.

Psychoanalysis, for a similar problem, may have taken years or, may not have been resolved at all. It was essential to be able to find the initial sensitising event which is always in the unconscious mind and never consciously remembered

She continued to get better and two years later she is well and regularly practices "self-hypnosis".

She is happy, both socially and in her marriage, and has never ever thought of suicide again.

Fear of Driving

Diagnosis: Death Expectancy Syndrome

Mary said, "every time I'm in a car with someone else I get into a real state". She described a typical anxiety attack. When she drives herself there is no problem. The anxiety only occurs when someone else is driving. It started about four or five years ago but was becoming progressively worse. The past six months were the worst. When driving in a car with someone, her husband or anyone else, she is constantly 'steering' and putting a foot on the brake pedal in her imagination. She understood that it probably was a fear of dying.

A word association exercise was not particularly helpful, but the following responses were of value.

Fear – car.
I fear – crashing.
If I crash – I may die.

Regressions.

The Prenatal and birth experiences were satisfactory. The *initial sensitising event* occurred at the age of two. She regressed to being in a bomb shelter during the Second World War. There was a lot of crying and moaning and there was a fear that she

7

may die. *The symptom producing event* occurred while on holiday with her mother and brother some years later. She was knocked down by a motorcycle, but made an uneventful recovery. When asked to go forward to the next experience that contributed to the problem, she was 12 years old. She became agitated and tearful. She began shouting. "I'm in the house with my mother and brother. The blacks and whites are fighting, rioting in our street. I think they are going to get us and kill us". This was the time of race riots in England. This was *the symptom intensifying event* for *'The death expectancy syndrome'*.

Another *Intensifying Event* occurred some years later. She was with her brother and his wife. He was driving very fast and changing lanes frequently. She was quite sure they were going to have an accident and that they would be killed.

The *"weed in the garden"* as previously described, was removed.

When she was seen two weeks later she had been in the car a number of times with the husband, and there were no feelings of anxiety.

She started taking short trips with her friends and eventually was driving long distances with anyone.

She continues to be able to drive with anyone.

Needle Phobia

When Yvonne consulted me she said, "I have phobias for a lot of things ever since I was a child. The worst is needles". She had fainted on many occasions when she needed to have injections. She intended having a child soon, and felt that this problem had to be resolved before she could do so. She believed her fear was a fear of death. She had had a fear of dying for a long time. Just thinking that she may need to have *a needle* one day made her problem worse.

She was hypnotised and *Ideomotor signals* as described previously, were setup. Her responses suggested that the problem was protecting her from something; the fear of dying.

Regressions.

She had just been born and was in her mother's arms. She was aware of her mother's fear. Her mother had been pregnant before and the baby died just before birth. Her mother was afraid that she would die as well. She picked up on the fear of her mother and was in great distress.

Useful responses from the word association test were as follows.

Underneath it all – I am afraid of dying.
I nearly died when – I was a baby.

My problem protects me from – dying.
Needles mean – panic.
I panicked when – all my life.

During the word association exercise, she had spontaneous "*abreactions*".

An *abreaction* occurs when someone spontaneously regresses to an unpleasant memory and *relives it*. There is usually a lot of emotion including crying, sobbing and/or screaming and shouting. The patient may act out and even get out of the chair. To the untrained therapist this can be very traumatic and frightening.

The first, occurred in response to the word "*fear*".

The second abreaction was in response to the word "*mother*".

She was four months in her mother's womb. She sobbed uncontrollably. When she settled down, it was explained to her that the fear she was feeling was her mother's fear. Almost instantly, she had another severe abreaction. It transpired that the doctors had told her mother that she was not pregnant. Yvonne felt as if she did not exist or that somehow she was destined to die. This was the initial sensitising event for the '*Death expectancy syndrome*'. This fear of dying became associated with anything medical. This fear was reframed by getting her to accept the fact that she had not died and had been born alive. She was taken through the birth experience and asked to take a deep breath and to breathe it out slowly. She was then asked what that deep breath made her feel. She shouted, "I am alive'.

A script "The breath of life" was discussed with her while she was still hypnotised.

The script starts, "A while ago there was a fear that you may die, but you were born, and you are alive. Each and every breath that you take is a constant reminder to your unconscious mind that you are alive"

Further, she was told that if anything happened to make her feel bad in anyway, she was to take a few deep breaths and to say to herself, "I am alive".

She was feeling much better when the session ended.

At the following session *"Age Progression – Regression"* was done.

While deeply hypnotised she was age progressed to the future.

She was progressed to a time when her problem had been completely resolved. She was to imagine sitting in the doctor's office completely relaxed and comfortable after blood had been taken for testing.

She was asked to imagine having a cup of tea, and chatting calmly with her husband.

She was to lift the "yes" finger if she could imagine this positive situation. She was to lift the "no" finger, if she could not imagine the positive reaction. She lifted the 'yes' finger.

She was then **regressed** to approximately halfway through the procedure, and to notice how comfortable she felt. It was suggested that she knew for sure that all was going well, and that the rest of the procedure will be completed without incident.

Gradually she was regressed to sitting in the waiting room, waiting to be taken in and feeling relaxed.

Then she was regressed to being home getting ready to go to the doctor's office and feeling calm and relaxed.

Gradually she was *progressed t*hrough the various steps leading towards having blood taken without any discomfort or anxiety, and then to again imagine sitting having a cup of tea with her husband and feeling proud of herself.

Because the responses had been positive throughout this session, a CD of the session was made for her to listen to at home.

When she returned a week later she reported no fear of needles or doctors.

Twelve months later she gave birth to a baby.

I trained her to enjoy a comfortable labour using self-hypnosis.

She had a successful, almost completely painless labour.

Panic Attacks

Max was referred by his general practitioner with a history of panic attacks.

He was 70 years old, retired, and married to his third wife.

He described full-blown panic attacks. He had palpitations, sweating, severe anxiety, abdominal discomfort and a fear of imminent death.

He had been suffering from anxiety for approximately 45 years. It started in his 20s. At the time he had not recognised them as panic attacks.

He often woke in the middle of the night with a panic attack and had to wake his wife. She would help him by getting him out of bed, making a cup of tea and taking his pulse, while continuously informing him that it is getting slower. Thus, she would help him relax.

He said the problem was affecting his life in that he tended to avoid social situations. Sometimes, he had an attack while driving and was becoming afraid to drive.

He was beginning to 'fear the fear'.

He described his childhood as being mixed up. He said that he thought he had always been a little bit nervous about being left alone and remembers sleeping with the light on. He had been dyslexic and only learned to read and write properly in his 20s.

He was adopted.

He was handed over to his adoptive parents when he was 10 days old. He was put into care for a while, while his adoptive mother gave birth to his stepbrother.

His adoptive father was very caring. He was quite strict, but was a lovely man. He was not well and was not able to give them the attention and experiences a father would normally give his children.

He described his adoptive mother as caring and an extra-ordinary woman, very much ahead of her time. But unfortunately, she was not able to show affection and never cuddled him. He wished she would have been more affectionate.

He believes that his biological mother fell pregnant by his biological father, while she was married to some other man away at war. When he found out he told her to get rid of it. She did not.

At times he felt as if he were still a 12-year-old.

He was happily married, but because of his anxiety was unable to work, and his wife was the breadwinner. He constantly worried about finances.

He was not happy in primary school because of bullying. He felt exactly the same in high school and did not complete his high school education.

He has had 40 jobs in his lifetime. He said that he always got to a point where he wanted to do something else and left his job. He has had two businesses. One a failure and the other a success.

He was concerned that he may not be able to be hypnotised, and was surprised to realise that he had an excellent hypnotic capacity.

Before the session ended he was given a CD to listen to, to relax at home.

Next session.

He had been listening to this CD and found it very relaxing.

He was taught self-hypnosis.

Next Session.

The word association was not of any value.

There seemed to be some resistance to regression.

He was encouraged to allow the first memory that he had to come up.

He was 16 years old. The experience was scary, hurtful, embarrassing and created a feeling of shame and being out of control. He had just started a new job and was being initiated. Five men dragged him down, pulled his pants down and covered his genitals with grease, iron filings and glue. It was exceptionally embarrassing. Consciously, he has forgiven them because he knew it was a "normal" thing to do.

These were not regressions. They were simply conscious memories.

By allowing him to '*freely associate*' he spoke about being 24 and described using an electric drill while his hand was touching a basin. He was electrocuted and felt he was going to die. However, he managed to free himself and survived.

When he returned for the next session he appeared to be particularly anxious. He had recently had a severe panic attack. I decided to take him to a "*shredder room*", where he would be able to shed and shred anything he needed to get rid of into a chute of '*no return*'. He was told that whatever he put into that chute, would be removed from his mind as if it had never existed. He was also told this special room was in an area of his brain that was totally soundproof. He could shout and scream and curse as much as he wanted to. He could say all the things he had wanted to say to various people, but had never had the chance.

This part of the session lasted 40 minutes.

At the end of the session, he commented on how valuable it had been.

At the next session he said that he had felt on top of the world for about four days. His symptoms had decreased from 10 to 6.

He was taught to "*reject negative suggestions*" coming from his own mind and from others.

Again, he seemed quite pleased at the end of the session.

As an adult he had met his biological parents. His birth mother was very cold and he never saw her again.

He got on well with his biological father and saw him from time to time.

As he continued to be resistant to regressions it was decided to continue with 'Traditional Hypnotherapy'.

He was taught the "clenched fist" technique for controlling anxiety.

It was firstly suggested that he should think of a time in his life when he felt confident and strong, even if it was a fleeting experience. Then, he was asked to go back to the memory and to begin to feel the feelings. He was told to make a tight fist with his dominant fist. It was suggested that the tighter he clenched his fist, the more confident he would feel.

He was asked to let the feeling move up the forearm into the upper arm and into his body and mind, while he took three deep breaths.

The feeling of confidence would remain a "subconscious resource" whenever he needed it.

All he had to do when he needed to feel confident and anxiety free, was to make a tight fist and all those feelings of confidence and freedom from anxiety would return.

Next, he was asked to think of a recent time when something happened that made him feel anxious.

When he was thinking of it, he was asked to make a tight fist with his non-dominant hand and to allow the feeling to drain from his mind into his fist. When he had all the feelings there, he was to open the fist and let the feelings evaporate into the air. He was then to instantly make a tight fist with his dominant fist, and become aware of the strong confident feelings.

When he returned for the next session he said that he had been using the "clenched fist" and that it had given him some relief.

The next time he was hypnotised, he spontaneously regressed.

He was cold, outside and wrapped in a blanket. He was confused.

He felt he was being held by a lady that he did not know.

He was crying and she kept him warm and made him feel better. Once he was indoors being held and loved he felt better again.

He was amazed at the memory and there were tears flowing down his cheeks.

After reframing this experience, using the adult 71 old ego state to give him valuable information, he reported at the next session that his anxiety levels had dropped from 10 to 3.

He continues to feel well and the last time he called he said that he was no longer reacting, but rather acting from strength.

Sometimes, it is not possible to do formal Hypnoanalysis. There is no reason why one cannot revert to traditional therapy.

Severe Anxiety

Charles aged 51, said he had been anxious most of his life. It became worse when his father died a few years ago. It felt as if he was in a continuous" flight response". Because of the severe anxiety he was unable to concentrate for more than a minute or two, and it stopped him from working. While we were discussing his childhood he said that his father had an occupation which necessitated him moving very often. As a result, he changed schools frequently. In spite of that he said that his childhood had been 'fantastic'. He often felt as if he were still very young. The most disturbing experience of his entire life was the death of his father a few years ago.

During the first attempt at inducing hypnosis he was very anxious and was not able to respond effectively. He was given a CD that would relax him, to listen to, at home. It took a number of sessions to get him to relax sufficiently to start therapy. However, eventually we were successful in doing so. The "fight or flight response" was finally discussed with him and we agreed that he was indeed in 'a continuous fight or flight response". Further, I explained to him that chronic ongoing anxiety was caused by a 'fear' that was experienced at some time, and had not been worked through at the time. It then became unconscious.

The word association exercise revealed that he felt stuck at the age of 13. Further, it revealed that there was a problem with death in that he was afraid of being alone when everyone passed. In addition, the word association exercise revealed that the problem went back to when he was a little boy.

Regressions:

The prenatal and birth experiences were both normal. When he was four years old he was playing in the garden and saw something scary. Initially, he thought it was a snake, but soon realised it was something else. He said, "I am riding my bike. My mother runs out of the house in a panic. I become scared and terrified. She takes me into the house and pacifies me". This was the *initial sensitising event* for his fear. When he was eight he was at a new school feeling scared and ashamed. It was his first day, and as usual he felt uncomfortable because he knew no one. He was ashamed of not being able to make friends easily. By the time he would make friends he would have left school. This was *the symptom producing event* for his fear. The *symptom intensifying event* occurred when he was 13. It was a scary event. It was afternoon, at home and the whole family was there. For some inexplicable reason he suddenly became afraid of his parents dying, and started crying. Now, he not only feared having to make new friends, but was beginning to be afraid of his parent's death and his own. He was wondering who would look after him when they died? His mother spoke to him about death and dying but he never understood.

Charles and I had a long discussion about death and dying, and eventually he understood that death was not only natural, but that it was indeed important. If no one, including animals and the flora never died, life would not be able to continue. For life to continue there had to be death.

When his father died 10 years ago his fear was intensified by the thought that he was now his 88-year-old mother's carer.

He was unable to get over his father's death. He was told to imagine being deep in the ground, sitting on a rocking chair and looking at his father's coffin. He was to imagine speaking with his father, telling him how much he missed him and loved him. He was also to listen to what his father had to say to him. He said goodbye to his father.

He was gradually brought up a flight of stairs to the "surface", and back to life.

The removal of the "weed" in the garden of his mind was done in a similar way to the previous cases. There was a lot of emotion and a lot of tears while he was removing the weed. At the next session he mentioned how upset he had been by all the memories that had surfaced. He was still a little concerned about what would happen to him when his mother died. The script whereby he was to, "*Confront his fears*" was worked through. He was also taught to end thoughts about anxiety. In addition, he was taught to 'reject negative suggestions' coming from his own thoughts and from the words of others. At the following session his anxiety had decreased from 10 to 2. He called a month later to say that he was still feeling well and that he was thinking of looking for work. He would contact me again, he said.

Tremor

Rebecca was 74 years old when she consulted me.

Her neurologist referred her to learn how to control stress, anxiety and the emotions that contributed to her tremor.

She suffered from a long-standing benign essential tremor that was causing problems for her. She told me that the shaking of the hands was her biggest problem. She had enjoyed doing patchwork and needlework but the fine motor control was steadily decreasing as a result of her shaking and she was no longer able to thread a needle properly. To relax she used to make embroidered cards for her friends and was frustrated that she was no longer able to do so. As her self-confidence waned so her frustration increased and made her shakiness even worse. She used to love cooking but was unable to do so.

The most disturbing experience of her entire life was the death of her father when she was eight years old. She had a very close relationship with him. She believed that her mother was jealous of their relationship. She was often not allowed to speak to him.

Hypnosis was induced and she was given a CD to listen to at home for further relaxation.

At the next session she was taught self-hypnosis.

Medical hypnoanalysis was explained to her and she wished to explore the possible causes of her anxiety and stress.

Regressions.

Prenatal experience.

There was a feeling of being unloved and unwanted. She said, "it feels as if I was not supposed to be here".

She felt guilty for being there.

The script 'Life, the purpose is you', was used to reframe the prenatal experience.

I noted that while she was hypnotised there was no tremor in her hands.

When scripts are used they are modified to suit a particular situation and/or a particular patient.

Subsequent regressions.

The prenatal experience was reviewed. I regularly review previous regressions to make sure that there are no residual emotions.

On review she said she still felt unwelcome by her mother. This was reframed by asking the 74–year–old ego state to communicate with her.

When she was three years old she was in the garden with her father at the Canary cage. She was chopping hard-boiled eggs to feed the Canaries. Her mother made some excuse to call her away. She felt hurt because her mother never wanted her to be with her father. She said, "mummy must really have loved daddy, because when he was killed she really mourned for him".

Spontaneously, she said, "Mommy frequently beat me over the legs if she thought I did not do something right. She had a large strap and beat me often. "I can still feel the pain". She said that when her mother came back from work, after father had died, the tea had to be ready. If it was not she was beaten. In addition, the Twin's bath had to have been prepared.

She then said that she felt as if she was 15 years old and that she was very angry with her mother. Her mother had behaved in this terrible way toward her ever since her father died.

She was asked to imagine her mother seated in a chair somewhere in the room.

When she indicated that she could see her, she was allowed to express the anger and resentment she had kept inside for so long.

There was a tremendous outpouring of emotion for about 15 minutes!

After she had expressed her anger, a script whereby she forgave her mother was worked through.

It was explained that the forgiveness was not for her mother, but for herself, so that the hurt and anger would no longer eat at her.

The next session.

'The Television Set Technique' of regression was introduced.

She was asked to imagine sitting at home in front of the television set.

She confirmed that she could imagine it by lifting her 'yes' finger. She was told that the television set had as many channels as what she had had years. She was to imagine that in her dominant hand she had the most sophisticated, state-of-the-art TV control.

With this control she could look at any channel. She could bring the picture closer or recede it to the back of the TV.

The screen can be split into 6 and she can look at multiple screens.

The video can be run forward and backwards. In addition, the video can be edited.

When she opens a particular channel she will see an image of herself at the age corresponding to the channel. The child or adult could communicate in two ways.

The child in the video could continue showing what was happening, or she may choose to talk to her about what was happening. She was told that *Channel 0* would represent her mother's womb. When she opened a selected channel, or one that she would choose, she was to lift the 'yes finger', to say what channel she was looking at, and to describe what was happening.

She would see or experience negative memories that needed to be worked with.

Channel 7.

She said, "dad has gone. He has been killed on his pushbike. He ran into a friend of his during a blackout at the army base, and went over the handlebars". She was upset at not being allowed to attend his funeral.

I asked if she wanted to say "goodbye" to her father. This was done as has been previously described.

Channel 13.

Her mother was remarried and she liked her stepfather.

She said, "I could never love him as much as daddy, but I do like him and I call him Pop-Pete".

She was never allowed to go anywhere without taking the twins with her. She was still receiving the beatings from her mother.

Channel 31.

Her mother had had a nervous breakdown and had been in a mental institution for six months. All the above experiences were reframed.

At the next session, she was very happy within herself. She felt more peaceful and was coping easily with her chores.

Since her last visit she had created 10 cards by hand.

She was thrilled at being able to thread a needle again and was delighted that the tremor had decreased.

She had not been able to create so many cards for a long time.

She was also able to iron her husband's shirts. Something she could not do before.

She was not ready to do the cooking yet, but, "my husband prefers doing it, anyhow".

Repressed anger turns inside and can affect every bodily system; the immune system, endocrine glands, sympathetic and parasympathetic nervous system, all mediated by the subconscious mind.

Ego State Therapy

I will describe two cases that were successfully resolved in one session.

Infertility

A colleague asked me to see a patient who had been trying for pregnancy for two years. All investigations were normal. She had undergone three failed attempts at IVF. (In vitro fertilisation.)

He had heard I was doing hypnotherapy and was wondering whether teaching her to relax would in any way improve her chances of falling pregnant.

Cynthia was a very pleasant lady with a bubbling personality.

Hypnosis was easily induced.

Ideomotor exploration, as previously described was setup.

I asked, "Is there a part of the personality that is preventing Cynthia from falling pregnant?".

The 'yes' finger moved.

I continued, "is the part willing to communicate with me?"

The 'no' finger moved.

'Parts' are often reluctant to communicate because there is a fear that one wants them to leave, die or change something they don't want to do.

The 'part' was reassured that I understood that it was part of her and that it was probably protecting her, and that I did not want the part to leave, die or change.

When enquired as to whether it was now willing to talk with me, using Cynthia's voice, she responded that she would.

I asked whether she had any particular name she would like me to call her. She said no. We agreed that I would call her 'protective part'.

I then asked, "what are you protecting her from?'

Her exact words were "bugger him".

She was de-hypnotised so that I could speak with her consciously.

I asked her to tell me about her relationship with her husband.

She said that they had been married previously. She wanted a child and he did not. For that and other reasons they divorced. However, two years ago they remarried and she had been trying to fall pregnant ever since. Because the IVF treatments were very expensive they had decided to stop.

She was re-hypnotised.

I asked the *protective part* to communicate with me again and said, "are you stopping her from being pregnant to punish her husband?".

The response was "yes".

I then said the following: – "I know that you mean well for her and that you are protecting her in the best way that you can. However, do you realise that you are 'cutting her nose to spite her face?'

She really wants to be pregnant and by punishing him you are punishing her as well?

I said, "With the information I have given you, would you be willing to let her fall pregnant and then to continue protecting her during her pregnancy and after?"

The 'part' agreed to do that.

After a month, she was pregnant and eight months later delivered a beautiful baby boy. They were both happy.

My colleague who had previously been rather sceptical, and only asked me to see her as a last resort, changed his mind about hypnotherapy.

Lost money.

A colleague, Colin, called and asked whether I could help him retrieve some money that he had misplaced.

I told him that we could try, but that I could not promise that we would be successful.

He told me that a friend had asked him to keep $10,000 for him while he was away.

Without telling his wife he hid the money in one of his drawers.

He and his wife had decided to go away for the weekend. Because the cleaner would be coming while they were away he decided to put the $10,000 in a safer place.

Recently, his friend had asked him to return the money but he could not find it.

He was hypnotised.

Ideomotor exploration was setup and I asked whether there was a part that knew where the money was.

The answer was 'yes'.

When asked whether the part was willing to tell me, or to let Colin know, where the money was, the answer was 'no'.

I asked what needed to happen for him to be willing to allow him to find the money.

The part said that if he told his wife what he had done, and apologised to her, he would be informed as to where the money was.

I wondered whether this would work.

That evening he called and told me that he had apologised to his wife. He then found the money on top of the wardrobe.

He said he would never have thought of looking there.

Fear of Sickness

Della, a 25-year-old primary school teacher told me that she had a fear of vomiting and a fear of anyone else vomiting. In addition, she had a fear of anyone being sick.

She had the problem as long as she could remember.

Her anxiety is aggravated if someone vomits or even say they are feeling sick.

If she is in the classroom and one of the children gets sick, she has a compulsion to leave the class and does not return until she is absolutely sure that the room has been thoroughly cleaned and that there is no possibility of infection. Being a primary school teacher this is becoming a problem for her.

She believes that when she is cured she will be happier, enjoy life more and be less paranoid about vomiting and also not be afraid of anyone getting ill. She described her symptoms as being 10/10.

She loves her work.

She had a happy childhood and has an excellent relationship with her parents who are divorced.

Three years ago she had a cholecystectomy, in the belief that it would cure her. As expected it made no difference.

The rest of the history was non-contributory.

After she was hypnotised she was taught self-hypnosis.

She practised regularly.

When she was five there was a scary, hurtful experience which made her feel 'guilty' and sad.

She was crying because her father was leaving home. It was scary and sad and she felt very guilty.

During the reframing it was explained to her that children often feel guilty in situations such as parents getting divorced. She was to understand that it was not her fault and had absolutely nothing to do with her. She accepted that and was willing to let it go. This experience *did not contribute* to the problem.

The initial sensitising event was at the age of four. It was a scary experience that caused guilt and sadness and was associated with being alone. It was night-time and she was alone in her room feeling sick. She was in her bed and had been vomiting. She was sad because it was in the middle of the night and she was on her own and unable to fall asleep. She cried until her mother came. Her mother changed the sheets and took her to her room, where she slept the rest of the night

The symptom producing event occurred when she was 12.

She was playing outside on her own. She had been sick the whole day. She vomited at school and was sent home. She said, "I am sick and I am afraid of vomiting again".

The symptom intensifying event occurred when she was 18.

She had her first experience of the fear of vomiting. She had just returned from a music festival feeling sick and vomiting. She was afraid.

The '*weed*' in the garden of her mind, as previously described, was removed.

At the next session she said that she was feeling a little better and she was no longer as stressed as she had been. However, when the children cough in class she still has to leave the room.

A script whereby she was to *end thoughts about anxiety* was read to her.

A week later she was feeling better and her symptoms had decreased to about 6/10.

On review there were no remaining subconscious memories contributing to the problem.

So it was decided to teach her to "reject negative suggestions" coming from her own thoughts and from others.

When she returned for the next visit she said that she had found it particularly useful and had been using it frequently.

Her mother said that she had noticed that her symptoms were much better. She was not responding in the way that she used to, when there was talk about illness.

However, Della felt that there was still a lot of work to be done.

A script whereby she was to "listen to your symptoms" was used.

This allowed her to communicate with an image of herself and to answer certain questions about her experience.

She was asked to describe how the image looked and felt and she said, "I got used to seeing the image. It became just like a picture with less feeling attached.

She had asked the image, "why do you make me so nervous and uneasy?". She was told to "walk away, and let the anxious feeling leave you".

A script whereby the unconscious mind was to continue doing *'what needed to be done'* at a subconscious level followed.

She was asked to write a story about a successful day. It would begin in the morning getting ready to go to school and would end with having had a pleasant successful day.

It was edited and divided into sections. I wrote it so that it started when she was at home with her partner, reflecting on the successful day and how she felt about it. The script was read to her.

She was taken back in time to when the bell rang and the school day had ended. Next, she went back to when the school day was halfway over. One of the children had complained of not feeling well and informed her about it. She had responded calmly and spoke to the child without getting upset. She told him to go to the toilet because he said his tummy was sore, and to come back when he was ready.

She was regressed to when the day was about a quarter through. One of the children had complained of feeling sick and nauseous. She reassured the child, without any anxiety. She was feeling confident and knew that the rest of the day would be successful.

Eventually, she was regressed back to when she had just woken and was preparing to go to school knowing that all was well and she was feeling confident.

Then we *progressed from* waking up and driving to school.

She was next progressed to being quarter through the day, and then through the various stages of the day ending with her being at home and reflecting on how wonderful the day had been.

A recording was made for her to listen to frequently.

When she returned she said that she was feeling very well. She now described the symptoms as being a 2/10.

Recently, she had been to the cinema and saw a movie in which someone was vomiting. Previously, she would have run out of the theatre and not come back.

This time it had absolutely no effect on her.

She said she would continue listening to the tape and that she was sure that did not need further therapy.

Rejection

Separation Anxiety Syndrome
Death Expectancy Syndrome

Felicity said that she had felt rejected all of her life. The fear of rejection is worsened when she knows that someone is going to leave, and is relieved by knowing that someone important is not going to leave.

As a child she had been repeatedly left by her mother. Her mother left home quite frequently and then would return. Eventually, she left for good when Felicity was 13 years old. Her parents divorced.

The children remained with the father.

After a while he could not cope and 2 of the girls, there were 4 of them, were sent to a home for children and remained there for some time.

She said that this fear of rejection consumed her and that she was continuously anxious.

She was not particularly happy in her marriage and started a relationship with someone at work.

She knew it could not last, and the thought of him leaving her had consumed her thoughts day and night.

She had an awful childhood. She said, "it was not a place I wanted to be in".

When I asked her whether she had ever felt as if she were still a child, she said, "only when I feel I am going to be rejected".

In her teenage years when boyfriends broke up with her she felt devastated and rejected. She found it difficult to cope with rejection.

Her mother left for the first time when she was 4 years old and she regards that as the worst thing that ever happened to her.

The responses from the word association exercise suggested that it all started when her mother left. She hated her mother for leaving and had been in *pain* ever since. It felt as if she was still three years old and was stuck there.

At the prompt, "All my life – she responded with, "I have been in pain".

I noted visible tears and she started crying. The pain she had was obviously emotional pain.

I decided to do *"An Affect Bridge"*.

An *affect bridge* is done in the following way.

While the patient remains deeply hypnotised she is encouraged to intensify the feeling, and when it has been sufficiently intensified she is told that I will count from one to 10 and she will go back *over a bridge of time* to the very first experience in her existence where this emotion was being experienced. She would feel what she felt then and would experience what she had experienced then.

She said, "I am in my cot. I am 11-months-old. I am on my own and my grandmother is sitting nearby. I want my mom".

She had been left with her grandmother because her mother was going to hospital to have a baby. She did not know that. She disliked her grandmother. She felt that if she was left there she would die.

Eventually her father came and fetched her.

While trying to reframe this experience the 'older part' of her was reluctant to give her the information required to be able to let go of the experience. However, after some persuasion she agreed to give her the information and the experience was reframed.

When she was three years old and her father could not cope with the children, she and her sister were left with the lady who had a son that she intensely disliked. She would often hide from him. Her sister who was one year older than her constantly protected her. She even ate her food when Felicity did not want to eat, so that Felicity would not be punished.

She was afraid because she did not know where her mother was. There was a feeling of impending death.

When she was four she was with her sister in the bakery that her father worked in. Mother had left again and had taken the two youngest girls with her.

Again there was a feeling of impending death.

The initial sensitising event was when she was 11 months. The symptom producing event occurred at 3 and the symptom intensifying. event was when she was 4 years old.

There were many other intensifying events – branches of the weed.

When she was 13 years old her mother left for good.

Additional intensifying events occurred when she was 14 and 16. She attempted suicide after she had broken up with a boyfriend.

The anger she felt toward her mother was resolved by giving her the opportunity to 'express' her anger by destroying a *Rock* on the top of a mountain far away from everyone. The rock looked like her mother and was infiltrated with all the hurt and anger she had felt.

While destroying this rock, by hitting it with a large hammer, she could express the hurt and anger she had been bottling up. She was told that she could scream and shout, and say the things she had been keeping inside all the years, because no one would hear her out there in the mountains.

The *"weed in the garden"* was removed as previously described.

It was an enormous weed with a lot of large branches.

The seed, root and all the branches were burnt.

She said, "I feel free now". The fear of impending death was gone.

She felt as if she was in control of her emotions and no longer feared the relationship breaking up.

Fear of Heights

Sally, 50 years old, said that she had been afraid of heights as long she could remember.

Recently, while visiting a local park she was unable to enjoy the flowers to the full because she could not walk over a bridge.

She did not remember much about her childhood. She has no problem flying.

She said that when she is cured she will be able to walk over bridges, climb ladders, and do anything else she wants to do that involved heights.

The rest of the history was non-contributory.

Ideomotor exploration resulted in a part responsible for the problem being willing to communicate. However, she was not willing to regress to the experience responsible for the beginning of the problem. At the following session there was a willingness to do so.

She was regressed to what she thought was the beginning of her problem.

About two years previously she and her husband were in a cave while on a group tour. It was dark. She could not see anything and had a tremendous fear of falling.

This fear was intensified using the 'affect bridge' as described previously.

She was five years old in kindergarten. She felt sick and was sitting on the roof of a car in the playground.

She had been put there by the class teacher for photographs to be taken.

She was afraid that she may fall off and injure herself.

Her mother had said not to climb on things because she would fall and hurt herself.

A negotiation with a "resistant parent ego state" occupied almost a complete therapy session. Eventually, the 50-year-old 'ego state' agreed to remove the memory.

At the next session there appeared to be total resistance to any regressions.

The unconscious mind was given the opportunity to make a decision as to whether it was willing to cooperate.

I said, "I respect the unconscious mind and I respect your decision to refuse to look at subconscious memories. However, as long as you continue refusing to look at unconscious memories Sally will never get better.

I am going to give you an opportunity to make a decision as to whether you would be willing to look at memories either now or in the future.

I will lift your right arm and as I count to 3 your arm will become rigid and stiff. If the unconscious mind wishes to continue avoiding looking at memories, the arm will remain rigid. If, however, the unconscious was willing to look at memories the arm will flop down onto your lap or the armrest.".

The arm remained rigid, indicating severe resistance.

This was an interesting situation. During the initial induction she commented on how relaxed she had felt.

Now she said she felt irritable and unable to relax.

I attempted to teach her self-hypnosis. It seemed to be working quite well. However, when I asked her to practice in the office she said, "I cannot do it".

She was asked to consider whether she wished to continue with therapy. If she wished to continue she was to contact me.

I had given up any idea of working with regressions and decided to use *"traditional hypnotherapy"*.

Hypnosis was easily induced.

The fear was *removed* using a *"balloon"* method.

She was asked to select a balloon, in her imagination, from a number of balloons lying on a table near her. She chose a blue one.

She was asked to put her fear into the balloon and when it was all there, she was to seal the balloon and allow it to float upwards. She was to watch the balloon disappearing into the stratosphere carrying the fear with it.

I noted some emotion. Again, using ideomotor exploration I enquired as to whether unconscious mind was willing to look at unconscious experiences. This time, it was willing.

The initial sensitising event occurred when she was one-year-old and her father was playing with her and throwing her up in the air and catching her. There was a fear of falling.

Interestingly, she mentioned that she had never really known her father and as far she could remember he had never taken notice of her.

She was disappointed that she did not know that he had indeed paid attention to her. If she had known that she may have been more kindly disposed towards him. This was reframed.

At the following session the *television regression technique,* as previously described was used.

When she was five she was playing alone in the playground at school and was feeling very sad. The other children were playing with one another but no one played with her. She said that the teacher had come over to her and told her that she had

45

been very naughty. She did not know what she had done and why the teacher said she was naughty. She smacked her, picked her up and put her on the car.

She then said, "she did this because she knows I am scared. She did that to punish me. I do not know why she thought I was naughty. She will not tell me."

Previously, she had not described the incident in full.

There appeared to be no other experiences relating to the problem.

She did, however, return to the one-year-old experience of her father throwing her in the air.

She abreacted, and said she was afraid of falling and hung on to my forearm. This was the Initial sensitising event and was reframed.

On occasion removing the *initial sensitising event is all that is required*.

When she returned the following week, she hugged me and told me how wonderful she was feeling. On the previous Sunday she and her husband visited the park and she had no fear walking over the high bridge.

Therapy was terminated.

Walking Zombie Syndrome – Spiritual

Ponce De Leon syndrome

When 26-year-old Elizabeth was asked what the problem was she said, "thoughts, intrusive thoughts".

When asked how long she had the problem she said "Since I stopped taking drugs and stopped drinking".

She had taken almost every description of recreational drug available. When she was in rehabilitation nine years ago, she stopped taking ice. Three years later she stopped the rest of the drugs.

She occasionally smokes weed.

She is living with her boyfriend, Robert. He had called and asked me to see her urgently. They have been together for three months. They had met on 'social media'.

They got on well but often argued about her jealousy, insecurity and her feelings of neglect. She felt that these feelings were not justified and was concerned as to why was she behaving this way

She was sure that they came from her feelings of worthlessness.

Her mother constantly told her how useless she was and that she was worth nothing. She grew up believing that.

She had a problem as long as she could remember.

She started drinking at the age of 15 and was expelled from high school after one year. She started using ice when she was 17. She believed that it all started because of the way she felt about herself, her life and her appearance.

She feels worse when she is alone and thinks about where she is going in life.

She feels better when, "I am being good to myself and having fun with Robert".

The problem was affecting every aspect of her life.

She believed that when she was cured she would be happy and would stop her addiction.

Previously, she had said that she was no longer taking drugs.

I asked what addiction she was referring to?

The addiction was to 'feeling pain', she said.

She often thought about committing suicide.

Her childhood was violent. Her mother is an alcoholic. So was her stepfather. Her mother and stepfather would often be violent with one another as well. Both of them abused her physically and mentally.

She had very little contact with her biological father because her mother somehow managed to obstruct her finding him.

A few years ago she found him and spent some time with him but there has not been much communication since.

She knew her mother had an awful childhood. She believed that was probably why she beat her.

I asked if she knew anything about her mother's pregnancy with her. She said that her mother did not want her. Her mother told her that she was beaten by her then partner throughout the pregnancy.

Elizabeth had four terminations of pregnancy without regret.

She has had chlamydia and gonorrhoea. Both have been completely cured.

When she was five she *died emotionally*. She has never felt truly alive. She felt as if she just existed.

It still felt as if she was still five years old. She was bullied in high school.

She had started drinking and was quite a rebel before being expelled.

At 17 she attempted suicide.

She has not attempted suicide again.

She has no religion but believes there is some 'Power'.

She has had many sexual partners. She never experienced any pleasure before meeting Robert.

She grew up believing her mother was abusive to her because she deserved it. Her mother had constantly told her how worthless she was. She has an excellent hypnotic capacity and was given a USB containing a relaxation CD to listen to at home. It was suggested that she should listen to it daily.

Next session.

The *word association test* was done while hypnotised.

Relevant responses were.

Anxiety – fear.
Useless – me – since – forever.
My mother always – yells.
Desire – love.
It started when – forever.
Sex – bad.
The real problem is – everything.
All my life – I have tried.
I could never do anything right – for my mom.
I regret – hurting people.
I really hate – myself.
As a child I – was scared.

I became – better when I left.
My father wanted – to love me.
My mother wanted – to hate me.
My sin was – abuse.
It all started when – I was hurt.
It got worse when – I thought – about – my mom.
Self-image – horrible.
Unwanted – me.
I am afraid when – I get angry.
I feel most guilty for – hurt.
Punishment – all the time.
I am being punished for – nothing.
I am being punished by – my mother.
My real age is – 10.
My chronological age is – 26.
Sometimes I think I am still – young.
I am really stuck at the age of – five.

Next session.

She was depressed and somewhat angry. She did not know why she was angry, or who she was angry with.

In previous relationships, anger took over after a while and she would terminate the relationship. She was beginning to get angry with Robert.

He is extremely kind to her and she really loves him.

I thought it was time to talk to her about *"safety in adult life"*.

Briefly, the script explains that because she had been abused as a child she viewed most people as if they were the abusers. She understood that Robert had not abused or harmed her.

I thought it was imperative to discuss the "*Hole in the soul* "with her.

She was asked to hold the little girl that she had been, on her lap and to hug her. She was to reassure the little girl from the past that she would always be there for her, and that she would never abandon herself again because she has a problem.

Her childhood was terrible and she developed a feeling of "shame".

She was told that there was a difference between guilt and shame. If you break something you feel guilty, but if the messages you keep getting are that you are not worthwhile and that no one loves you; that creates a hole in the soul.

She needed to *re-parent* herself. She was to become a loving parent to herself.

As a result of her upbringing she could only feel good if someone else, or something else, made her feel good about herself by what was done to her or with her.

Inside she had always felt, "I am useless – I am bad".

She understood that the reason she had become sexually promiscuous was to find the love that she sought.

The alcohol and drugs 'anaesthetised" her feelings of self-hate.

To fill the '*hole in her soul*' she was asked to say, "I love me". Initially, she found it difficult. Eventually, she was saying it clearly and loudly.

She was told that in future if anything happened to upset her, or to make her feel bad about herself, she should take a few deep breaths and say the words, "I love me".

A sense of peace would fill her mind. Further she was told the she would frequently be repeating the phrase consciously and unconsciously.

When she returned two days later, she commented on how well she was feeling.

She had been saying, "I love me" frequently, not because it was necessary, but because it just 'came up'.

Regressions.

The prenatal experience

In spite of the fact that she had said that her mother did not want her, she said she felt 'warm and comfortable' in her mother's womb.

Initial sensitising event.

She was five years old and said, "I am in the house with my mother and stepfather. He is holding me upside down. He pulls my pants off and smacks me on my bum".

She felt helpless and embarrassed. Her mother did nothing. She just watched.

She continued, "why are they doing this to me?"

"Why are you hitting me?".

She had wanted to watch television and get some attention from her mother.

She said, "She never gives me any attention unless it is for something bad".

The "*Silent abreaction*"

She was asked to imagine a rock representing the anger that she felt toward her mother, as described in a previous case.

After destroying the rock, she was asked say to something positive about herself.

She said, "I am okay". She expressed a need to forgive her mother because she was much 'bigger' than her.

At the next session, three days later, she said that she was feeling much better and that she had been repeating the phrase, "I love me" frequently. In addition, the voices in her head had stopped and for the first time in many years her head was silent.

A script was used to assist her to forgive her mother.

She was taught self-hypnosis, and was asked to send a list of positive affirmations. They were to be *"statements about the future, made in the present as if they had already happened"*.

They would be corrected, if necessary, and a recording would be made so she could listen to her own suggestions.

She was told that when she listened to the suggestions, they would sink deeply into her mind, and would have a profound effect on the way she felt, acted and behaved.

She was asked to think about the suggestions and to let me have them when she had written them.

I suggested a minimum of 30 and a maximum of 50.

Cutting loose.

At the following session she informed me that she had been practising–self-hypnosis and was working on her list of affirmations.

Her mother had called that morning to ask when she was moving out of the home that she was sharing with Robert. She was nagging her to move out, "because she does not want me to be happy".

I felt that this was a toxic relationship and that it was time to cut loose from her mother.

A script called *"The song and dance"* describes the relationship with parents, and how it affects the children.

A script, "*Cutting loose from an unloving mother*" was worked through.

She remarked on how well she was feeling and that she realised that she was beginning to change.

Her relationship with Robert was excellent. They were going away for a week and she would see me again when they returned.

At the next session I felt it was appropriate to work through her childhood and to resolve the parts of her that remained behind as a child

A "Ponce De Leon scan" was done.

The analogy *of a motorcar on an assembly line* was described.

If one or more, workers do not turn up for work on a particular day the part or parts, that should have been added would be absent.

So, when the car comes off the assembly line it will not be complete.

It would have to be taken onto the assembly line again, and the part or parts, would have to be added at the right place where they belonged.

Only then would it be complete and ready to drive.

It was suggested that there were parts in *the assembly line of her life* where parts of her had remained behind, isolated and alone. It was time for those parts to become integrated with her, where they belonged.

The youngest part remaining behind was five years old. Her stepfather was hurting her.

When she was 10 she had lice in her hair, and instead of using a special shampoo, her mother, against her will, shaved her head completely.

At 13 she had a black eye because her mother had punched her.

When she was 17, her mother left the family and she felt alone.

She was asked to hug each of the parts individually, and to tell them that she was from the future and was willing and able, to care for them.

She was to ask the parts if they would come with her into the future?

They all agreed, and she took them by the hand and walked up a path towards the summit of a mountain.

As she walked up all of them became integrated with her where they belonged.

When she was standing on the plateau of the mountain, with all the parts integrated, she was told that, that like the car, her personality was now complete and that each part was in the place where they belonged.

The plateau represented the beginning of a new life. [='

She was asked to imagine a childhood *as it might have been; as she would have liked it to have been.*

She was to indicate "yes" when she was able to do that.

The unconscious was asked whether it would be willing to seal the *fantasised memory of childhood,* as if it were really the childhood that she had had.

There was agreement.

The following suggestion was made – "you will now, and in the future behave, act and react as if that fantasised memory was the actual childhood you had".

She was taught to *"reject negative suggestions"* coming from her own thoughts and from others.

She was to recognise, reject and positively reaffirm any negative suggestions.

The affirmation CD had been made and was given to her to listen to.

A week later she informed me that she had been mistrustful of Robert. There was no particular reason.

I spoke to her again about *safety in her adult life* and not to confuse the abusers from the past with the present people in her life. She was very happy at the end of the session and said that she had needed that.

At the next session she spoke about how well she was and how happy she was in her relationship.

She was practising self-hypnosis regularly and listening to the affirmations frequently.

A script, "*believe you are alive*" was done.

When she arrived for the last session she was looking absolutely amazing. She was no longer the depressed woman that I had seen originally. There was a spring in her step, she was dressed brightly and was smiling a lot. She said that she no longer felt as if she just existed. She knew that she was alive.

Changing Memory

John told me that he had a problem concerning his work. He has to fly quite often and because of his problem he was unable to do his work properly.

He said that when waiting to board a plane he became slightly anxious, but when he was on the tarmac and ready to board, he had to turn around and quickly go to the toilet many times before he could board his plane. He usually flew back in the evenings, and he had the same problem on the way back.

Lately, he was beginning to have the same problem driving to work and was compelled to stop at the home of strangers and asked to be allowed to use their toilet facilities. This was most embarrassing.

A technique of regressing to before the symptoms began was used. While hypnotised he is told that I will count backwards from his present age towards the age before his symptoms began. After every number that I count he will become younger and younger and will feel as he felt at that particular age. When he reaches the age before his symptoms began he is to lift the 'yes' finger.

John was 37 years old and signalled 'yes' when he was 34.

The verbalisation went as follows, "you are now 34 years old and you have no problem whatsoever. You're feeling well and comfortable. Is that correct?

He signalled 'yes'.

I continued, "I'm going to count slowly forward from your present age and when you reach the age where something happens that contributes to your problem that 'yes finger' will float up again.

The finger lifted when he was 35. He was asked to review that experience at a subconscious level and to bring it to consciousness. When he indicated that he was now consciously aware of the experience, he was asked to talk about it.

It was a Saturday morning and he had an appointment to see a physician in a medical building.

After the consultation he felt a need to defecate. For some inexplicable reason every toilet on the floor was closed and he could not gain entry.

It was becoming urgent and he noticed a broom cupboard. He opened the door. It was filthy and dirty. There was nothing he could do about it, and he defecated on the floor.

He drove home feeling most upset and his symptoms started almost immediately. It became progressively worse until he decided to come for therapy.

Using ideomotor communication as previously described, unconscious was asked whether it was willing to change the memory of that experience. It was agreeable.

I then said, "you have just left your physician's office. He told you that all was well. Suddenly, you had a desire to defecate and you found a very clean, well-kept bathroom. An attendant welcomed you and you did what you had to do. You washed your hands and feeling quite pleased with experience and the reception, you gave the attendant a tip and left. You drive home comfortably".

Unconscious was asked to replace the previous memory with the imagined one. It agreed. He was then told, "from this moment on and into the future you will find yourself acting and responding as if the memory just described to you was indeed experience you had".

The symptoms disappeared and never came back.

A similar case

Rebecca said she was unable to enter shopping centres. As a result, she was unable to do shopping for the family and for herself. When she entered a centre she would stop, turn around, run back to her car and go home.

It transpired that on a visit to the shopping centre, some months before, she had a desire to defecate and could not find a toilet. (bathroom) She decided to go home. While driving home the urge became uncontrollable and she soiled herself and the car. She was unable to return to any shopping centre.

As in the previous case unconscious agreed to change the memory and I said to her, "you have just finished a most enjoyable and successful day of shopping. You have purchased everything you need. You have a desire to defecate and you find a clean toilet on the same floor where you had been shopping. When you entered the first thing that struck you was how clean and well-kept it was. You washed your hands and used a little Eau de cologne that had been placed at each basin. You found your car in the parking area and drove home comfortably. It had been a very successful outing and you are looking forward to your next shopping experience."

Unconscious accepted changing the memory.

She has had no problem shopping ever since.

The two cases demonstrate how simple and rapid therapy can be when the unconscious is willing to cooperate.

Insomnia

Insomnia is a very common complaint. Sometimes, no cause is found but often a subconscious cause exists.

I'm going to describe a few cases in which a cause was found.

Amy said she had a long-standing inability to sleep throughout the night. She falls asleep easily but wakes after a few hours. She was 50 years old and the problem started in her 30s.

The problem is aggravated by anxiety, bird noises and even the sound of the wind would wake her. As usual, she had tried "everything" before coming to see me.

Ideomotor exploration suggested that the ability to sleep through the night was due to fear. A part responsible for the problem communicated that it was protective and had been with her "from the beginning".

Regression to conception brought up an emotional fear coming from the conceptus and from the mother. A fear of what may happen; a fear of an anticipated struggle to survive. In addition, there was an awareness that she may be uncared for. There was also an awareness of a fear of being unwelcome.

During the birth process there was an unwillingness to be born because of the doubt as to whether she would be cared for or wanted. She felt stuck and was aware of being pulled out. Probably a forceps delivery.

Soon after birth she felt alone and she said, "I am lying my crib and no one is there. It hurts. I do not cry because it hurts to cry. I am hungry. I do not know where my mother is. I feel deserted".

Those experiences were reframed using the 50-year-old ego state.

On reviewing those experiences at the next session there are still feelings back in the uterus because of the 'realisation' of the whole struggle ahead.

Again the 50-year-old assured the unborn baby that she would care for her and nurture her, and that in spite of everything that happened she was alive and she had survived.

The one-year-old felt guilty for having inhibited the birth process.

When she was two her brother was born and she felt totally rejected.

Extracts from the word association exercise: –

father – harsh.
It all started when – I was born.
It got worse when – brother was born.
Mother – not there.
When my brother was born – felt abandoned and lost.

I regret – not being ready to be born – as a result of which – I
 messed it all up.
My birth was – traumatic.
It all started when – I was born.
It got worse when – I separated from my husband.
The real problem is – I am alone.
I have been alone since – I was born.
I'm really stuck at the age of – 10.
My problem will be resolved when – I stop worrying so much.

The concept of the 'Separation Anxiety Syndrome' and the
'Walking Zombie Syndrome' were explained to her.

The *seed – 'initial sensitising event'* was her birth and when she
felt abandoned on day one.

The '*root – 'symptom producing event'* was the birth of a brother.

A '*Symptom Intensifying Event'* was when she was sent to boarding
school. The rejection by her parents and finally, the separation
from her husband were also symptom intensifying events. The
separation from her husband was the last straw for the *'Separation
Anxiety Syndrome'.*

The removal of the 'weed' was done as in previous cases and a
script describing her zest for life was done.

She started having more 'good nights', but she tended to forget
to do her self-hypnosis. An affirmation CD was made for her.

A month later *at her request* the PDL scan was repeated. In the
uterus, the unborn baby was still feeling mother's anxiety and

fear. This was once again reframed. She agreed to leave that in the past.

Gradually, her sleep pattern continued improving.

Christine. Age 41.

She complained that because of their inability to sleep she was irritable and ratty. She had had the problem for many years. When she was 15, she was aware of the parents constantly fighting. When she was 17, her father attempted to shoot her mother. Soon afterwards he committed suicide. Initially, there was a sense of relief because there was no longer the fighting and shouting.

Ideomotor exploration discovered that there was a 'part' responsible for the inability to sleep. The part was protecting her from the possibility of her father killing her whilst asleep. The part was 17 years old. The adaptive function was reframed using the 41-year-old ego state to reassure the younger one that she would care for her, and that it was no longer necessary to protect her by keeping her awake and aware. She sleeps throughout the night.

Penelope. Aged 23.

She said, "I have trouble falling asleep". It started when she was 15. Previously, she had slept well and could not think of any reason why she would now not be able to sleep.

Ideomotor responses revealed the following.

The insomnia serves a purpose in the unconscious mind. An ego state, calling itself, "no sleep" keeps her awake. It does so to protect her from dying. 'No sleep', came into existence when she was five years old. She had been sitting with her parents watching television and overheard her parents talking about a lady that had died in her sleep. When she was 15 she heard that, her grandfather had put his hand through a glass door and she was afraid that she would die.

I asked the ego state whether it was willing to consider protecting her in other ways than keeping her awake. The three ways that were suggested by unconscious, were accepted and the part was willing to protect her in those ways. It would keep her calm, keep her out of dangerous situations and keep her away from bad food.

The ego state agreed to protect her this way for a period of a week or two, to see whether it would be effective in protecting her, other than keeping her awake. If it was effective, it would then continue to protect her in that way forever. She now sleeps through the night.

Ponce De Leon Syndrome

Jennifer had a problem with self-esteem. She believed that her childhood was responsible for the feelings. I asked how her life would be different when she was cured and she said that firstly she would be 'free' from the pain that had been present forever, and secondly, she would have confidence in herself again.

She described her childhood as 'sad' and went on to say that she had always been unhappy about her childhood. When I enquired as to what was the part of a childhood that she felt so sad about she said, 'most of it, I think' and she started crying.

Her mother had been unhappy during the pregnancy with her and apparently had been suicidal at the time. Jennifer was born prematurely and was unable to breastfeed.

She often felt as if she were still five years old.

She never had a good relationship with her parents, who divorced when she was 13. She said that when she had been in school she never received help or assistance from her parents.

She volunteered that she had a problem with self-esteem from her early childhood and she often felt shame about, 'being myself'.

Prenatal experience.

It felt as if she was full-term and ready to be born. There was a feeling of being, 'sad and unsafe'. In addition, there was a feeling of hopelessness and helplessness. She accepted that those were probably her mother's feelings and not her responsibility. She was willing to let the feelings go.

PDL regressions.

In view of the fact that her symptoms seemed to relate primarily to her childhood, it was decided to do the PDL scan as previously described.

The youngest part that remained behind was a few days old. She was feeling hurt, afraid and angry. She was alone. No one was holding her, and she felt as if no one cared.

She was willing to go with her into the future and as she started up the hill towards the next part that had remained behind, the little baby of a few days old became integrated and a part of Jennifer where she belonged.

The next part was approximately three months old. She felt worthless, alone and separated from love and warmth. She said there was not enough warmth for her.

The next part that remained behind was 5 months old and was feeling lonely. As before, there were no feelings of warmth or love. She had been left alone and was untouched by anyone. She felt like a piece of rubbish that had been discarded. A few times she repeated, "it feels like I am discarded like a piece of rubbish because of what I am like – I am rubbish. It feels like rubbish because no one cares for me".

The two parts described above were willing to go with her to the future. She took them by the hands and started walking up toward the next part that remained behind and they also became integrated with her, where they belonged. The, "*hole in the soul*", as previously described, was done. She was able to say, "I love me".

She was not willing to look for the next part that had remained behind. So, the session was terminated.

She cancelled the following session because she felt vulnerable.

Next session.

She had previously sent a list of affirmations and a CD had been made for her. This was given to her. She had been using self-hypnosis successfully and effectively. She felt that there was no need or reason to look at any other past experiences.

I didn't feel that the problem had been completely resolved, but had to accept her feelings about it, so therapy was terminated.

Overeating

When asked what the problem was Lucy said, "I just feel too chubby". She described herself as 'an emotional' eater.

When asked how long she had had the problem she responded, "probably all of my life". From the Medical Hypnoanalysis perspective, this would suggest that the initial sensitising event was probably before birth.

She realised she was not obese. She simply wanted to get rid of excess fat in her abdominal area. She weighs 78 kg at present and would like to lose about 5 kg. She said she was unable to diet and that she was not an "exercise person".

She was wondering whether Hypnosis would be effective in helping her resolve her problem.

Her mother had a difficult pregnancy with her. During her birth there was a cord around her neck and she was born prematurely.

The rest of the history was non-contributory.

She has an excellent hypnotic capacity.

The next hypnotic session.

Regressions.

The prenatal experience was perfectly satisfactory. She felt warm, wanted and loved.

During the birth experience she said with emotion, "it feels like I'm choking and I am going to die. I need to get out of here. I can't and I'm going to die"

She was taken through the birth process and was told to take a deep breath as she felt herself being born. She did this. The suggestion was given, "each breath that you take will be a constant reminder to your unconscious mind that you are alive and that you did not die".

The following suggestion was made, "a short while back while you were being born there was a feeling that you may die, but you did not die, and you are alive. You don't need food of any kind to prove that you are alive. If anything happens to upset you in any way, you will no longer have to eat. Each breath that you take is a constant reminder that you are alive. So, all you need do when you become upset is to take a deep breath and repeat to yourself "I am alive".

Suggestions concerning the correct way of eating were given. It was suggested that there would be a compulsion starting from deep inside of her mind to put her utensils down when there is food in her mouth. She is only to lift her utensils and prepare the next mouthful when she had enjoyed and swallowed the food that was in her mouth.

I explained that if she ate in this manner, and enjoyed her food, messages would be sent from her stomach to her mind telling the appetite centre that her hunger had been satisfied and that consequently she would eat less and be satisfied with less food.

An 'age progression' was done whereby she was taken to 'sometime in the future' where she has become the person she wants to be, and has lost the mass she wished to lose.

She was asked to imagine herself looking in a mirror, in the nude, and to see herself looking and feeling the way she wished to look and feel. Using ideomotor communication she indicated that she liked what she saw. She was asked to dress and to describe what she was wearing.

There was a smile on her face as she confirmed that she liked the way she looked.

She was told that as she looked in the mirror she could reflect on what needed to happen for her to achieve the figure she now had. It was suggested that firstly, she had learned how to relax and secondly, she had been eating in the manner described in the previous paragraph.

She was regressed back to the present time, and while remaining deeply hypnotised, the suggestion about correct eating was reinforced.

Before she left she mentioned how real the image was and how delighted she felt that she looked exactly as she always has, but she did not have a chubby abdomen any longer. She was also amazed at how real the birth experience was, and how the emotions had welled up.

Comment

The Birth Experience, birth anoxia syndrome, could have been the initial sensitising event for the walking zombie syndrome. However, she had no symptoms to suggest the diagnosis.

Even though one may experience an initial sensitising event that could possibly lead to any of the syndrome's discussed in the introduction, nothing happens unless there are subsequent experiences creating the same emotion.

The triple allergenic theory is confirmed.

I hope that having read the 15 cases I have described I have given you some idea of the place and value of *Hypnosis* in Clinical Practice in general and *Medical Hypnoanalysis* in particular.

About the Author

Dr Jules Leeb practised as a general practitioner in a small country town for 10 years before specialising in OB/GYN. While practising as a specialist he became interested in hypnosis for Labour. He attended courses and 'fell in love' with hypnosis and hypnotherapy.

He successfully delivered over 3000 patients who used self-hypnosis as the only form of pain relief for their labours. He also trained patients for his colleagues.

Since 1993 he spent his professional day practising OB/GYN in the morning and Medical Hypnoanalysis in the afternoons. He retired from OB/GYN practice in 2002 and migrated to Perth Australia from Johannesburg South Africa.

He still practices hypnotherapy daily at the ripe old age of 85.

He derives immeasurable pleasure from the honour of having had the opportunity of changing so many minds for the better.

He had the honour of being the Vice President of the South African Society of Clinical Hypnosis from its inception in 1980 until 2000.

He has taught courses in Hypnosis in Ireland, Australia, and in England, for the Royal Society of Hypnosis. He has lectured and been a keynote speaker at Hypnosis Congresses. Until his retirement in 2002 he was a member of the *International Society of Hypnosis*, the *South African Society of Clinical Hypnosis*, an *Associate Member of* the *American Society of Hypnosis* and of the American Academy of Medical Hypnoanalysis.

Printed in Great Britain
by Amazon